ALLIGATORS & CROCODILES

A PORTRAIT OF THE ANIMAL WORLD

Leonard Lee Rue III

TODTRI

This book was designed and produced by
Todtri Productions Limited
P.O. Box 20058
New York, NY 10023-1482
Fax: (212) 279-1241

Printed and bound in Singapore

ISBN 1-880908-21-2

Author: Leonard Lee Rue III

Producer: Robert M. Tod
Book Designer: Mark Weinberg
Photo Editor: Edward Douglas
Editors: Mary Forsell, Joanna Wissinger, Don Kennison
Production Co-ordinator: Heather Weigel
DTP Associates: Jackie Skroczky, Adam Yellin
Typesetting: Command-O, NYC

PHOTO CREDITS

Photographer/Page Number

Peter Arnold, Inc.
S. J. Krasemann 7 (top)
Kevin Shafer & Martha Hill 33 (top)
Roland Seitre 11 (bottom), 19, 52, 53, 54, 55
Myrna Watanabe 21 (top)
Martin Wendler 12 (bottom), 33 (bottom) 35 (top & bottom), 36, 37, 40-41
Gunter Ziesler 16 (top), 34 (top & bottom), 39 bottom, 70 (top & bottom), 71 (top & bottom)

Bullaty Lomeo 21 (bottom), 26

James H. Carmichael, Jr. 4, 20, 31, 51, 64, 65 (bottom), 69

Doug Cheeseman 39 (top)

Dembinsky Photo Associates
Stan Osolinski 6, 15, 29, 47 (bottom)
Dusty Perrin 27
Fritz Polking 12 (top), 13, 18 (bottom), 58 (bottom), 59
Mark J. Thomas 11 (top), 44

Innerspace Visions
Doug Perrine 7 (bottom), 16 (bottom), 28 (bottom), 30, 45, 66, 67, 72 (left), 77 (bottom)

Joe McDonald 8 (left), 10, 17, 24-25, 32, 42, 60 (top & bottom)

Nature Photographers Ltd
E.A. James 65 (top)

Leonard Lee Rue III 14

Bruce Shwedick 56-57, 62 (bottom)

Gail Shumway 22, 23, 43

Tom Stack & Associates
John Cancalosi 72-73
Jeff Foott 47 (top)
Chip Isenhart 74
Bob McKeever 76
Mark Newman 68
Brian Parker 8-9, 48, 49, 50, 75, 77 (top)
Wendy Shattil and Bob Rozinski 18 (top)
Robert Simpson 3

The Wildlife Collection
John Giustina 28 (top), 46, 78 (bottom)
Martin Harvey 5, 58 (top), 61 (top & bottom), 62 (top), 63, 78 (top), 79
Jack Swenson 38

INTRODUCTION

The gaping maw of this huge alligator is a fearsome sight, although the creature may be only attempting to cool off. The teeth are shed on a continuous basis, which explains why even adjacent teeth are of different lengths. The alligator is missing a number of teeth that have been shed and will be replaced.

The scream was loud and piercing, given by the young woman running the motor on our six-metre skiff, just as the bow dipped beneath the roiling, muddy waters of the Alligator River. The sound reached our other two boats. They turned and raced back to rescue us, none too soon. One of the fellows in the second boat snapped a photo that showed the head of a five-metre saltwater crocodile in the midst of our floating gear, looking for my two companions and myself. The huge croc bit into my life preserver and pulled it underwater, but all he got was the bun, no meat; I wasn't wearing the preserver, and for that I'm thankful. We were in Kakadu National Park in northern Australia, the area made famous by the movie "Crocodile Dundee". It is legendary for the numbers of the huge saltwater, or Indo-Pacific, crocodiles that inhabit the area. I was told by the locals that five people had been killed by crocs there in the last seven years.

The term "man-eater" has much to do with people's fascination and interest in these huge reptiles. We humans like to think

that we are at the top of the evolutionary ladder and most of us live far from the possibility of being eaten by some sort of wild creature. It was not always so. At one time, our ancestors were high on the list of prey species eaten by many of the large predators. Lions, tigers, bears, sharks, and crocodiles then, and occasionally today, consumed humans. The adrenaline charge that allowed our ancestors to escape these predators and survive is now gotten vicariously through the media coverage given to modern-day incidents by the newspapers and television newscasts. People are fascinated with that which scares them.

Actually, only a few species of these giant lizards ever became man-eaters; most do everything possible to avoid all contact with man. However, there is so much documented evidence of attacks on people by those few species that people assume all of these large reptiles are man-eaters. It is in an attempt to set the record straight that this book has been written.

Cuvier's dwarf caimans are the smallest members of the crocodilian family in the New World. They are found in the northern half of South America and seldom exceed 1.6 metres (5 feet) in length.

The Indo-Pacific, or saltwater, crocodile can function equally well in either saltwater or freshwater environments. Although they are usually found in coastal regions, they sometimes stray inland, going as far as fifty kilometres up freshwater rivers.

THE BEAST ITSELF

Prehistory to the Present

Alligators, caimans, crocodiles, and gharials are jointly referred to as crocodilians. The crocodilians are holdovers, survivors of that long-ago time known as the Age of Reptiles, a time when the dinosaurs were the ruling creatures on the earth, dating from 265 million years ago to roughly 66 million years ago. The dinosaurs, the pterosaurs, and the crocodilians were known as Archesaurians and, even today, the crocodilians are referred to as saurians.

At the end of the Triassic period, about 210 million years ago, a small, slim reptile appeared which has been named *Terrestrisuchus* and is thought to be the direct ancestor of our modern-day crocodilians. The *terrestrisuchus*, as its name implies, was primarily a land-dwelling reptile, running about on either two or four legs and feeding upon smaller lizards.

The ankle joints of these early reptiles are similar to present-day crocodilians. It is one of the main links between them that these creatures could also either crawl slowly, bellies close to the ground, with the legs bent outward away from the body, or the legs could be straightened, lifting the body away from the ground and allowing the creature to run very rapidly for short distances. A creature known as *Desmotosuchus* also evolved that was very crocodilian in appearance and had evolutionary adaptations to a life in water, such as a vertically flattened tail for propulsion and a secondary palate that allowed them to seal their throat to prevent water from entering their lungs when they opened their mouth underwater. Both of these adaptations are present in today's crocodilians.

By the end of the Jurassic period, about 146 million years ago, the ancestors of

Alligators are creatures of habit. When one finds a good spot above the water level where it can bask in the sun, it will return to that spot day after day.

present-day crocodilians had evolved, and although the direct lineage from that era to the present is not precisely established, both form and function were. It was also during the Jurassic period that the huge single continent, known as Pangaea, split apart to form the continents we know today. This continental drift caused some forms of crocodilians to become separated. It also caused the great divergence, through isolation, into the many different species that we have today as each species evolved and adapted to the conditions in which each was found.

There is great speculation about the events that brought about the extinction of the dinosaurs. The one most favoured is that a huge asteroid hit the earth, sending up clouds of dust that enveloped the planet, blocking the sun, which killed the plants that the dinosaurs lived on. A second theory, that the beginning of an ice age killed off the dinosaurs, is not generally accepted because most of the dinosaurs died at about the same

Turtles frequently climb up on an alligator or crocodile to bask in the sun, just as if they were on a log. This is risky because many of the crocodilians feed upon turtles.

Although this alligator and hatchling were photographed in the Everglades National Park, the vegetation is typical of the marsh and swamp areas in the southern United States. Large groups of fish, the alligators' main food, inhabit the warm waters.

Young crocodiles are precocial, or capable of a high level of independence from birth, and are not fed by their mother. They are nourished for a while after hatching by the remnant of the egg yolk in their stomach. They soon learn to feed upon insects and the small minnows that abound in the warm water of the swamp.

time. Another theory is that neither of these things happened, but the cooling of the earth was somehow speeded up. Since the dinosaurs were poikilothermic, or cold-blooded, a sudden drop in the temperature would not only have devastated their vegetative food supply, but greatly reduced their body functions and their ability to move. The crocodilians survived in part because they spend a large part of their time in water, which is more temperature-stable than air. There is also the possibility that many fish, which are the crocodilians main food source, survived by eating each other. There is also the probability that the crocodilians would have been able to hibernate, as our modern alligators do, during the winter months in the colder portions of its range, thus reducing their need for food for an extended period of time. Research indicates that a large crocodilian may be able to live for up to two years without eating. Climatic changes, such as the ice ages, shrank the ranges and greatly reduced the number of species of crocodilians. They are now found only in the tropic and subtropic regions of the world. The populations of the remaining species were greatly reduced by a burgeoning human population, which led to competition for habitat

The American crocodile receives complete protection as an endangered species in the United States, although it is still hunted for its skin in some of the Caribbean areas in which it is found.

and increased confrontation. A demand for the reptiles as food and their skins for leather led to the market hunting of many species. Many species were pushed to the brink of extinction. Some species survive today primarily in captivity. A growing awareness of their place in the web of life has spawned new laws and regulations that have allowed many of these ancient reptiles to replenish their numbers in the wild. The American alligator has increased its numbers so dramatically that it had to be removed from the endangered species list and be harvested on a regulated basis in some areas.

Head and Eyes

All four forms of crocodilians–alligators, caimans, crocodiles, and gharials–basically resemble each other. The alligator has a broad, rounded, shovel-like snout while the gharial's snout is long and very narrow. The snouts of the caimans and the crocodiles are between these two extremes, although a long, tapered snout is most common. All crocodilians have both their nose and their eyes located on the top of the skull so that they can see and breathe while the rest of their body is submerged beneath the water. Their eyes are set close together, giving them the binocular vision needed by all predators so they can accurately gauge the distance between themselves and the prey they must capture.

By regulating the amount of air in the lungs, these saurians can float on the surface or sink below the surface with just their eyes and nose protruding above the water. The

crocodilians have valvular, crescent-shaped nostrils that open when they breathe and close completely when they submerge. They have good hearing and their ears are covered with flaps to keep the water out.

Most of the species hunt primarily at night and have vertical, cat-like pupils that open wide to allow more light to enter in low-light situations. Since they are night hunters, their eyes have a layer of tapetum at the rear of the eye which reflects whatever light is gathered back through the pupil, doubling their ability to see in the dark. Because of the tapetum, the eyes of crocodilians glow in the dark when a bright light is shined on them. The eyes each have a transparent nictitating membrane that covers it when they swim underwater.

Most of a crocodile's teeth fit into grooves in the opposite jaw, so that the teeth are outside of the mouth when closed instead of being hidden by the lips, as is common with most other creatures.

This head-on view of a saltwater crocodile allows you to see how the base of the tongue completely blocks the entrance to the throat. This allows the crocodile to grasp its prey underwater without getting any water in either its stomach or lungs.

Note how the pupil of this caiman's eye has expanded to gather more light after dark. The pupil is contracting in reaction to the camera's electronic flash. It proved impossible to take a photo in complete darkness when the pupil was fully open.

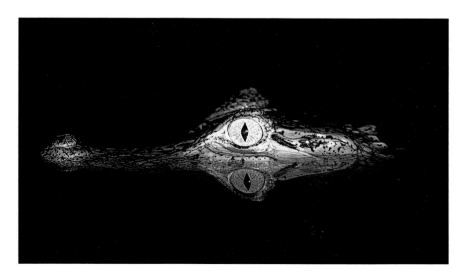

This dramatic photograph shows a Nile crocodile actually catching a Thompson's gazelle. The gazelle was evidently trying to cross the Mara River in Kenya when the crocodile ambushed it in the shallow water.

Feeding

All of the crocodilians have powerful jaw muscles to snap their jaws shut and to hold tightly to any struggling prey. The muscles to open the jaws are very weak and their mouth can easily be held shut. Their teeth are sharply conical, varying in length according to their placement, designed for grasping and tearing, with small prey swallowed whole while larger prey is torn apart and the pieces swallowed. The teeth grow in sockets and are shed and replaced periodically. Some old alligators have had as many as fifty sets of teeth.

Baby crocodilians feed heavily on insects and small fish, and then on larger prey as they become older, according to the species. In much the same way that birds use small stones in their gizzards to grind their food, large crocodilians swallow stones, called gastroliths, to help grind food in the stomach.

Like snakes, the crocodilians' digestive system is powerful enough to dissolve bones. When food is plentiful, these creatures store fat in their tails and body. This stored fat enables them to go for long periods without eating. As all crocodilians spend many hours each day immobile, their energy requirements are low.

Common caimans prefer the broad, flat marshland areas where fish are common and are the main dietary staple. Like all crocodilians, this caiman is an opportunist and will also feed upon whatever wading and water birds and small mammals it can capture.

The Nile crocodile is found over most of Africa, except for the northern desert areas and the southern mountain region. It lives up to its fierce man-eater reputation, killing a large number of people each year.

Body Temperature

Alligators can live much farther north than any of the crocodiles because they have the ability to hibernate for periods of three to five months during extremely cold weather. They usually dig chambers in a river bank that are at least partly above water, with underwater entrances. Some crocodiles will also dig such chambers, but they do so to escape from the heat of summer. As mentioned, crocodilians are referred to as being "cold blooded" when, in reality, their body temperature reflects the ambient air temperature or that of the nearby water.

These reptiles adjust their internal temperature by taking advantage of their surroundings. After hunting throughout the hours of darkness, the crocodilians crawl up on the sand bars or river banks as soon as the sun has dissipated the lower temperatures of the night. As the air temperature is warmed by the sun, these reptiles will open their mouth in a wide gape. The evaporation of the moisture of the large mouth area lowers the

Since alligators are poikilothermic, or cold-blooded, their body temperature is very close to the ambient temperature of the environment. Alligators usually remain in the water on cool nights because the water is much warmer. As the sun raises the air temperature, they crawl out of the water, as this one is doing, to bask in the sun.

Different creatures have different ways of lowering their body temperature in hot weather. Humans sweat, elephants flap their ears, dogs pant, and alligators gape.

The floodplain areas preferred by the common caiman often dry up during a drought. As this occurs, the caiman will dig holes in the mud and bury themselves, undergoing a period known as aestivation, until the rains replenish the water.

A saltwater crocodile crawls up a riverbank in order to bask in the sun. It will stay up on the bank until the ambient temperature raises its body temperature too high, then it will return to the water to cool off.

temperature of the creature's blood as it courses through the mouth. When the temperature becomes uncomfortably hot, the crocodilians will either seek the shade of nearby shrubbery or return to the water. Later in the day, when the heat has abated, they may crawl back up on land until the cooling of the evening air sends them back to the water to seek prey of some sort.

In times of drought, crocodilians gather in whatever holes contain water. Alligators, too, are famous for the holes they dig, which teem with concentrated fish, birds, and gators during periods of low water. Usually, crocodilians get along well with each other, although smaller members will get out of the way of the large ones. However, cannibalism does take place in some situations. Just recently, researchers saw larger alligators kill and eat two smaller 1.5-metre alligators in a pool near Gainesville, Florida. Over 212 alligators were concentrated in this pool because of drought.

All of the crocodilians appear to be very lethargic and slow moving, and they usually are. When they extend their legs, however, as this Nile crocodile is doing, they are able to outrun a man over a short distance.

The hind feet of the crocodilians are partially webbed, but their main propulsion, while swimming, is provided by their heavily muscled, vertically flattened tail. The tail is moved in an undulating S-shaped motion, driving the body forward at a speed that allows them to overtake swimming prey. While swimming, the front feet are held parallel to the body, pointed to the rear. When crawling about on land, the tail is dragged along the ground, leaving a well-defined trail. When a crocodilian runs on land, the tail is moved in the same S-shaped configuration used in swimming.

Fish, snakes, turtles, and even birds show their relationship to crocodilians through the scales on their bodies. Many of the reptiles shed their entire skin periodically as they outgrow it. The crocodilians shed individual scales. The skin of the crocodilians is heavily armoured over the top of the head, back, and tail. When a crocodilian is taken for its hide, only the skin from its underside is used for leather because that section does not have the projecting, ridged scales known as osteoderms.

Crocodilians communicate through four scent glands and through auditory grunting and calling. The American alligator is the most vocal of all, with the young gators grunting while the adults, both male and female, bellow. The bellowing can be heard at any time of the year, most frequently in April and May during the breeding season. The bellowing can be heard for a long distance and individual gators can be recognised by their bellow. Crocodiles and caimans may breed at any time of the year.

There is a slight webbing between some of the digits of the Morelet's crocodile. This is an aid to swimming, even though most of the propulsion in swimming is done by the crocodile's tail.

Body and Movement

It was long believed that the crocodilians used their strong tails to sweep their prey off its feet and into the water. It is now known that most of the prey is caught after a silent, stealthy stalk and a startlingly swift attack. Mammalian prey is seized and pulled underwater to drown before being torn to pieces by the reptile. Some crocodilians can actually gallop for a short distance in pursuit of their prey on land. They have been known to jump as high as one metre horizontally and some large ones can spring up vertically to a height of up to two metres.

The scales on the legs of a crocodile are smaller in size than those on its back in order to allow for greater flexibility in the limbs, which is needed for mobility's sake.

The ridged scales on the crocodilians are known as osteoderms, from osteo, meaning bone, and dermis, meaning skin. The bony ridges in each of these scales make this part of the crocodile's skin unfit to be used for leather.

Reproduction

Depending on their habitat, some crocodilians scoop out a hole in the sand or dirt using their hind feet to lay their eggs. Alligators pile up mounds of vegetation using both their mouth and their feet. Anywhere from thirty to fifty leathery-shelled eggs are deposited in the hole, which are then covered with sand, dirt, or vegetation. The sun provides the heat needed to incubate the eggs, with the rotting vegetation providing additional heat. The hatching time is greatly influenced by the ambient temperature, but most hatch within two to three months.

Alligators and some crocodiles stay in the vicinity of the nests to protect them from such predators as raccoons, bears, wild pigs, monitor lizards, and goannas. An interesting phenomenon was recently discovered in research on alligators. It was found that when the eggs were incubated below 32°C (90°F) mostly females developed. Above 33.5°C (92°F) more males were produced whereas, if the temperature was between 32°C and 33.5°C, both sexes would be pro-

Alligators build up huge mounds of vegetation in which they lay their eggs. The rotting vegetation and the rays of the sun provide the heat needed to incubate the eggs over the sixty-five or so days that it takes the eggs to hatch. Just prior to hatching, the young start to grunt. Upon hearing this, the female tears open the nest to allow the little ones to come out.

duced about equally. This phenomenon is called temperature-dependent sex determination, or TSD. Research with other crocodilians, as well as with sea turtles, shows that they are affected also, but at slightly different temperatures and with different results according to the species.

In order to escape from the leathery eggshell, baby crocodilians are equipped with a

Within a short time after hatching, the baby alligators will change colour, developing the greyish colouration typical of an adult. They may retain the yellowish stripes on their belly even when full grown.

Even though you can't tell how big they are, you can tell that this is a grouping of young alligators because they still have yellow markings on their backs and tails.

Upon hatching, the baby alligators are brightly coloured (we don't know why). They are about 19 to 25 centimetres (8-10 inches) in length and will grow at a rate of about 30 centimetres a year until they are five years old, when their growth slows dramatically.

projection of skin known as an "egg tooth". This is similar to the egg tooth of birds; the only difference is that a bird's egg tooth falls off on the third day while the crocodilians' egg tooth is reabsorbed on about the fifth day. The young crocodilians are strong enough to dig their way through the protective layers of sand, dirt, and vegetation.

Unlike the hard eggshell typical of most birds' eggs, the shell of an alligator egg is leathery. In order to cut through the eggshell, the baby alligators have an "egg tooth" on the top of their nose. Shortly after hatching, the egg tooth falls off, after it has served its purpose.

In alligators, there is evidence that the female is summoned by the babies' grunting and that she assists them by digging open the top of the nest. Both crocodile and alligator mothers have been seen carrying their young to water in their mouth. The young crocodilians are preyed upon by all of the above-mentioned predators as well as by snakes, fish, herons, and vultures.

Upon hatching, the babies are 19 to 25 centimetres (8-10 inches) in length and grow at the rate of almost 30 centimetres a year until the age of five. They will continue to grow all of their lives, but slow down progressively from then on. The length each species may attain is given in the account of that species.

Following page: Thousands upon thousands of the common caiman are taken each year for their leathery skins. Thousands of young caimans are sold each year in pet shops. This caiman's population is declining in Peru where it has no protection, but increasing in Venezuela where it is protected.

ALLIGATORS AND CAIMANS

The American Alligator

The American alligator, *Alligator mississippiensis*, is found from South Carolina to northeastern Mexico along the coastal regions and as far up the Mississippi River as Arkansas. Its range has been greatly diminished by the draining of both coastal and inland swamps and marshes when these areas were converted to farmland. Their numbers were decreased by market hunting and then further reduced by poaching in the 1950s and 1960s. The alligator was then considered endangered, but has recovered to the point where Louisiana estimates there are at least 380,000 of these big reptiles in that state alone. A hunting season had to be reinstated to prevent the overpopulation of alligators and the total destruction of the valued furbearers such as the muskrat, otter, and nutria.

The alligator feeds mainly upon fish and it has decided preferences as to which kind of fish it will eat. It feeds heavily upon many species of garfish, but will not eat the long-nosed garfish. It has very broad tastes,

A great egret keeps its distance from a young alligator. Alligators will feed upon the egrets and herons that share their habitat, but seldom get the chance to do so because the birds are exceedingly wary and keep a watchful eye on the gators.

Although fish is the mainstay of the alligator's diet, they also feed on the many turtles found in the marshes. This one has caught a soft-shelled turtle. The alligator's digestive juices are so powerful they can dissolve the turtle's shell and bones completely.

From below the surface of the water, you get a fish's-eye view of an alligator resting with just its eyes and nose visible. Alligators can float or submerge at any desired depth by controlling the amount of air in their lungs.

This alligator lies completely submerged at the bottom of the pool. Note how valves have closed its nostrils. The alligator's eyes appear opaque because the nictitating, or transparent, eyelid covers the eye, acting as "goggles" to keep water out.

though, and will readily feed upon any birds, snakes, frogs, turtles, crabs, or small mammals that it can catch. They have been known to catch and eat animals as large as a deer.

The largest alligator there is an authentic record of was the giant called "Old Monsurat", killed by E. A. McIlhenny of Tabasco fame on his Avery Island, Louisiana, estate in 1890. The huge gator measured 5.6 metres (19 feet 2 inches), but it was not weighed. It could conceivably have weighed in the 202 to 225 kilogramme (450-500 pound) range. There are a number of records of alligators in the 4.8 to 5.1 metre (16-17 foot) class.

I estimated that the largest alligator that I have personally seen was 4.5 metres (15 feet) in length with a probable weight of 160 kilogrammes (350 pounds). I saw this alligator in the Aransas Wildlife Refuge on the Texas coast and the refuge biologist said he thought my estimate was about right. Alligators have been accredited with great longevity, but research has found that most of those over

fifty years old have lost most or all of their teeth, so they would have great difficulty in obtaining prey species and would gradually die of malnutrition. In fact, McIlhenny was convinced that the huge gator he shot in 1890 was dying as it was practically toothless.

As the American alligator population has grown since the 1970s, and the areas the gators live in have been invaded by a burgeoning human population, conflict was inevitable. What has made the problem worse is that many people began to feed the gators, which not only attracted them but kept them in the area. Rather than shy and retiring, as a truly wild alligator is, the ones that are fed become very aggressive. Attacks on people are now fairly commonplace. Many pet dogs are eaten by the gators. The gators have to be removed from boat docks and from swimming pools. The ponds and lakes on golf courses are known as "water hazards" and many of them are now truly hazardous because alligators have taken up residence there.

This alligator slowly cruises the shoreline of a lake in the Everglades National Park, searching for food. Alligators can swim so stealthily that they don't leave a tell-tale ripple.

The Chinese alligator is believed to be the creature which the dragon of Chinese culture and religion is based upon. It has a shorter snout than its American counterpart.

The Chinese Alligator

The Chinese alligator, *Alligator Sinensis,* is believed to be the progenitor of the mythical dragon of Chinese art, literature, and religion. The alligator was first mentioned in Chinese literature in the third century AD. In his book on his travels, published in 1299, Marco Polo describes an encounter with what surely must have been this alligator while he was in China.

No one is sure just how extensive the range of this alligator was in the years gone by. Although it is mentioned in Korean literature, the waters are too cold and the rivers too swift and turbulent for this reptile. The range of this alligator today is along the banks and marshes of the Yangtze River in the area of Yueyang, Wuhan, and Nanchang. This area is on the 30th parallel, giving the Chinese alligator about the same range northward as the American alligator.

An aerial view of a group of alligators resting in a favoured location. The vegetation is worn down by the alligators' frequent passage.

Like the American alligator, its Chinese counterpart will hibernate during the cold winter months by submerging itself in a tunnel in the riverbank. Made lethargic by the cold, many of these alligators drowned in their burrows in 1987 when the Yangtze flooded in the winter. It is estimated that there are perhaps no more than three hundred Chinese alligators alive in the wild. Captive breeding programmes in zoos and research stations throughout the world are helping to keep the species alive. Although there are reports of these alligators growing to a length of 3 metres (10 feet), a really large one today is 2 metres (6.6 feet).

One favourable point for this alligator is that its hide is not desired for leather because of osteoderms on its belly. However, the Chinese attribute medical cures to different parts of its body, such as its gall bladder, and they also relish its meat.

This is a very shy, retiring species and there are no records of it ever attacking a person. It has been known to take villagers' dogs and chickens. It feeds primarily upon fish, frogs, and turtles.

The Common Caiman

The common caiman, *Caiman crocodilus*, is perhaps better known as the spectacled caiman, a name suggested by the bony ridges and light colouration encircling its eyes. It has a large range, being found from southern Mexico through Central America and on down through the heartland of South America's Amazon basin. There are no accurate figures on its total population, but it is estimated that there are at least four million of this species in just Venezuela. Years ago, baby spectacled caimans were a hot-selling item in pet stores. Records of some 3-metre (10-foot) specimens exist, but any spectacled caiman that reaches a size of 2.5 metres (8 feet) is considered to be a big one. It is hunted for its skin, despite having some osteoderms on its belly. Apparently none of the native people eat the spectacled caiman. If this caiman is exposed to cold weather, it changes colour from a basic greenish yellow to brown. In the brown stage, even the southern subspecies resembles the most northern subspecies, which is known as the brown caiman. The breeding season for this common caiman occurs in August at the tail end of the dry season. This is advantageous to the species because, by the time the eggs hatch out in November, the waterholes, swamps, and savannahs will be filled with water and teeming with aquatic life. The spectacled caiman is unique in that the females often nest communally, with two or more females laying their eggs in the same mound. This has the decided advantage of giving the nests greater protection, with two or more guardians. In spite of this increased protection, as many as 80 percent of the nests may be opened and the eggs eaten by the large monitor-type lizard known as the tagu. Despite the fact that this caiman is common throughout so much of a large range, very little is known about its eating habits. It is known that it feeds upon fish, small invertebrates, and small animals. Although they are found in ranching areas, they have not been known to eat livestock.

The spectacled, or common, caiman is a medium-sized crocodilian with an adult averaging about 2.5 metres (8 feet) in overall length. Occasionally one is reported to be 3 metres (10 feet) in length, but this is extremely rare.

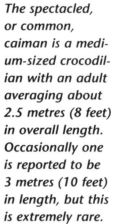

The anacondas are the largest snakes in the world, with some attaining a length of up to 10.5 metres (35 feet). Here a yellow anaconda has killed a common caiman. The trident bone in the snake's jaw will allow it to open its mouth wide enough to swallow the caiman whole.

In extremely hot weather a caiman, by the process of metachrosis, will become lighter in colouration, which serves to reflect the sun's rays away from the body so that the caiman does not become too hot.

Where food is plentiful, the spectacled caiman is very tolerant of others of its own kind. They can be seen sunbathing in large numbers in a very small area. When food becomes scarce, they become much more belligerent and aggressive, killing and feeding upon each other.

The Amazon River basin is extremely rich in all types of brightly coloured butterflies. Here two different species are resting on the head of a common caiman.

Common caimans have the ability to change colour in response to cold weather. As the weather turns cold, the caimans become darker in colouration, allowing the body to absorb more of the sun's rays to warm them. This is known as metachrosis.

The Broad-Snouted Caiman

The broad-snouted caiman, *Caiman latirosteris*, is found in southeastern Brazil, Paraguay, Uruguay, and Argentina. It can be recognised by its broad snout and by the ridge that runs the length of the snout. This caiman closely resembles the American alligator in appearance, but not in size. A really big individual may attain a length of 1.8 metres (6 feet), but this is rare. It is a very shy creature and usually inhabits areas with dense floating vegetation, making it extremely difficult to see. They are basically aquatic and usually hunt at night. They feed mainly upon snails and crabs, as well as many types of aquatic invertebrates. It is thought that their broad jaws are an adaptation to allow them to crush the shells of the turtles they feed upon. They are the southernmost species of caimans and, as such, are exposed to colder weather than are their more northern relatives. Their dark colouration helps them to absorb and to hold more warmth from the sun even on cold days. Although they are more cold-tolerant than are other caimans, they spend less time basking on the riverbanks and more time in the water.

Unfortunately for the survival of this caiman species, its skin makes especially fine leather and is much in demand. Hunting has greatly reduced its population. In addition, it is believed that many of these caimans may be dying from parasitic flukes that they pick up by eating the snails that their hosts discard.

The male broad-snouted caiman helps the female dig the nest, helps to guard the eggs, and has been seen carrying the hatchlings to the water in his mouth. There does not appear to be any concentrated effort to prevent the depletion of this species.

Broad-snouted caimans are the southernmost crocodilians found in the New World, ranging as far south as Argentina. Because it lives so far south of the equator, this caiman is exposed to more cold weather and seldom basks on riverbanks in winter. Water is a more stable environment and, by staying in the water, the caiman can control fluctuations in its body temperature to some extent.

It is believed that the wide jaw of the broad-snouted caiman is an adaptation to crush the shells of the many types of turtles upon which it feeds. They also feed upon snails, crabs, birds, and small mammals.

The Black Caiman

The black caiman, *Melanosuchus niger*, is concentrated in the Amazon River basin, Guyana, and French Guiana. It is the largest crocodilian in South America. Really large ones can reach a length of over 6 metres (20 feet). The black caiman has been in great demand for its skin, and market hunting has reduced both its population and range by about 99 percent. In the early 1970s, as many as 66,000 hides were shipped out of Colombia alone. Today, this caiman is virtually extinct in that country.

The young black caiman feeds heavily upon shrimp and crabs, snails, and fish. As they grow larger, they tend to feed more upon mammals, such as the capybara, the world's largest rodent, as well as on deer. Fish are still an important item in an adult's diet, as are turtles. Black caimans have especially good hearing and often home in on their prey, in the darkness, by detecting whatever sounds the prey makes. They eat domesticated animals and, occasionally, one will attack a human. The attack on humans is a comparatively rare event.

In December, drought conditions concentrate fish in shallow pools, creating an almost unlimited food supply for the caimans. This allows the female to be in excellent condition when she does her egg laying and they lay between fifty and sixty-five eggs. The nest is about 1.5 metres (5 feet) across and up to .75 metres (2 1/2 feet) high, made of piled vegetation.

As they are very tolerant of each other, a number of females will often build their nests in a very small area. With a number of females in a small area, predation is kept to a minimum. The black caiman is in direct competition for some food sources with the spectacled caiman, whose range it overlaps and which is much more numerous. The tremendous reduction in the number of black caimans has had a deleterious effect upon the environment. Both the piranha fish and the capybara populations, black caiman food staples, have increased dramatically as the black caiman population has declined. The capybara are destroying agricultural crops and piranha are attacking more cattle.

The largest of all caimans, the black caiman may reach a length of up to 6 metres (20 feet). These caimans are most common and grow to their largest size in the vicinity of Kaw in French Guiana. Overall, their population has been reduced by about 99 percent in the past one hundred years.

Black caiman feed mainly upon fish, although they also prey upon animals as large as capybara and deer. An important item in their diet is turtles, such as these seen basking on the same log as the caiman.

Following page: In December of each year, as the rivers and lakes start to dry up, the caimans gather in areas that still have water. As all of the fish are also gathered in the same areas, they feast upon an unlimited supply of food.

The Dwarf Caiman

The Cuvier's dwarf caiman, *Paleosuchus palpebrosus*, has the thickest skin of any of the crocodilians. They are also the smallest in size of any of the New World crocodilians, with a big male reaching perhaps 1.5 metres (5 feet) while the female grows to 1.2 metres (4 feet) or less. It is thought that these caiman might have thicker armour as added protection due to their small size, but it may also be a selective adaptation to protect them from being cut when thrown against sharp rocks in the fast-flowing water in which they often live. I tend to believe the former hypothesis because these caiman spend a lot of their time in still waters and they also spend much time on land looking for food. Those that live in still water frequently have filamentous algae growing on them. This provides them with an even better camouflage.

These caiman are found in Brazil, French Guiana, Suriname, and Venezuela. The Cuvier's caiman feeds heavily on fish, but also takes shrimp, crabs, frogs, toads, snakes, birds, and small mammals. Cuvier's caiman are shy and usually solitary. They have never been populous and no one really knows how many there are. They are not sought for their hides. The female builds her nest out of vegetation, then adds mud to finish the heap. The nest is usually further hidden under some dense vegetation and is seldom hit directly by the sun. Because the ambient temperature is never as warm as the sun's rays, it takes up to ninety days for the twenty to twenty-five eggs to hatch. The female stays in close attendance to the nest to guard it from predators and to open the mud-hardened structure when the young break out of their shells.

The Cuvier's dwarf caiman has a very short, comparatively broad snout. This caiman's body is also more heavily armoured than most crocodilians as a protection against being injured when dashed against the rocks of the fast-moving rivers it inhabits.

The Schneider's dwarf caiman, *Paleosuchus trigonatus*, is frequently called the smooth-fronted caiman because the skull lacks the bony ridge between the eyes. Both Cuvier's and Schneider's caimans have a bony flap that comes down, completely protecting the eye, when the upper eyelid is lowered. Like the Cuvier's caiman, the Schneider's caiman is also very reclusive, coming out only under the cover of darkness. They spend the day-time hours hidden in tunnels they excavate in the riverbanks.

This species of caiman prefers to live in fast-flowing or turbulent water. Their diet is mainly fish, with a large number of those being different kinds of catfish. They have also been known to eat snakes, shrimp, crabs, and snails. They occasionally hunt on land for birds and small rodents. One of these caiman, 1.8 metres (6 feet) in length, was eaten by an anaconda that measured 5.9 metres (19 1/2 feet) long. Some of these huge snakes have measured up to 10.5 metres (35 feet) in length and many of them prey upon the smaller crocodiles.

A large male Schneider's caiman may measure up to 1.7 metres (5 1/2 feet) in length while a large female may measure 1.4 metres (4 1/2 feet).

The Schneider's dwarf caiman is not hunted for its hide because its belly is also covered with osteoderms, rendering it unfit for leather. The ventral osteoderms do provide this caiman with a complete set of armour. The nest is constructed by the female out of vegetation. The female then lays a clutch of between twelve and fifteen eggs. As with the Cuvier's caiman, it takes almost three months for their eggs to hatch.

Note the elliptical pupil in the eye of this Cuvier's dwarf caiman. Creatures with such eyes usually hunt at night. As daylight fades, the pupils' slits expand widely, allowing more light to enter, giving the creatures superb night vision.

AMERICAN AND AFRICAN CROCODILES

The American Crocodile

Because it has the largest range of the four New World crocodiles, the American crocodile, *Crocodylus acutus*, is perhaps the best known. In North America, its range is restricted to the brackish regions of the Florida Keys, although it goes up fresh water canals around the Everglades. It is found on islands in the Caribbean, Mexico, Central America, Colombia, Venezuela, Ecuador, and Peru. A distinguishing feature of all of the crocodiles is that the fourth tooth, on either side of the lower jaw, is so long it protrudes through holes in the upper jaw. The American crocodile can further be distinguished from all other crocodiles because it has less bumpy osteoderms on its back. It is extremely rare to find any specimens of this crocodile today that measure over 4 metres (13 1/2 feet) in length. There are authentic records from years ago of some that were 7 metres (21 1/2 feet) in length.

All crocodiles have a gland in their mouth that allows them to extract and eject salt from saltwater so it can be drunk. This gland is more efficient in some species than in

The American crocodile is an endangered species in Florida, where this one was photographed in a saltwater mangrove swamp. Their population is higher in other regions of the Caribbean.

The crocodilians can control the depth at which they float by controlling the amount of air they retain in their bodies. Note how the eyes and the nostrils of this American crocodile protrude higher than any other part of the skull or body.

others. The glands of the American crocodile are among the less efficient and even the adults prefer to drink fresh water while their young must have access to fresh water in order to survive.

American crocodiles frequently dig tunnels to which they retire, not as a protection against the cold but as a refuge from the heat, during periods of drought. This is known as aestivation. Like alligators, the American crocodile will lumber up on land in the early morning to warm up and then retire to the water in midday to cool off. The crocodiles feed primarily at night. While young, they eat mainly small fish and some small vertebrates. The adult crocs feed mainly upon fish, turtles, snakes, small mammals, and small domestic livestock. Attacks on man have occurred but are rare.

American crocodiles seldom make a nesting mound. In the swampy areas where they live, the females, like turtles, use their hind feet to excavate a hole in the soft peat. She lays between forty and sixty eggs that measure 7.5 centimetres (3 inches) in length by 5 centimetres (2 inches) in width. The female will then make a tunnel for herself in the immediate vicinity so that she can guard against any predators. After a three-month incubation period, she will help the young to hatch by opening the nest.

The populations of this crocodile have greatly declined not only because it was hunted for its skin, but because dams and canals diverted so much fresh water from streams for agriculture that the salt content of bays and estuaries is too high for the young to survive.

The gaping mouth of this young American crocodile may be an attempt to cool off or it could be a threat gesture.

Anyone seeing the long, narrow snout of this American crocodile should not confuse it with the broad, shovel-snout of the American alligator. The range of these two species over-laps only in the southern Florida coastal region.

Caribbean Crocodiles

The Morelet's crocodile, *Crocodylus moreletti*, is found only on the Caribbean side of Central America. It is small as crocodiles go, with a really big one measuring up to 3.5 metres (11 1/2 feet) in length. Most of the big ones are in the 2-metre (about 7-foot) class. The colouration of this crocodile is a dull greyish brown, which helps it to blend in with the dense floating vegetation of the freshwater ponds and lakes that it frequents. In these areas, they feed upon snails, turtles, fish, and small mammals. The young eat many invertebrates.

Because these crocodiles lack osteoderms on their belly, their hides have been in great demand and market hunting has brought them to the verge of extinction over much of their range. Fortunately, they do breed well in captivity and Mexico is doing a fine job of captive rearing and releasing of the young crocs in the Yucatán area in an effort to prevent their extinction. Also, most of the countries where

Biologists fear that the Cuban crocodile will be bred out of existence through crossbreeding with the American crocodile which has invaded its range. The American crocodile has a much larger population.

The Morelet's crocodiles are not a threat to humans, but their populations have been greatly reduced by hide hunters. As these crocodiles breed and reproduce very well in captivity, a number of rearing programmes will ensure that they don't become extinct.

they are found have improved enforcement of the protection that the crocodile needs if it is to survive.

The female Morelet's crocodile will build a substantial mound of vegetation as a nest in which she will lay between twenty and forty-five eggs. It takes about eighty days for the eggs to hatch. The mother will be in the vicinity to prevent predation and she is sometimes joined by the male in caring for the hatchlings.

The survival of the Cuban crocodile, *Crocodylus rhombifer*, is seriously threatened because this species has the most restricted range of any of the crocodiles. It is found in only two swamps in Cuba. While formerly the American and Cuban crocodiles inhabited different ranges, the destruction of much of their natural habitat has forced the two species into the same areas. The Cuban crocodile has never been as numerous as its American counterpart and the two species are now hybridising to the detriment of the Cuban species. It is conceivable that, within a few years,

the Cuban crocodile could be bred out of existence. The Cuban crocodile has a much shorter and more broad head and is more yellow in colouration than the American, with the hybrid offspring often showing characteristics of both species. However, since the American is much more numerous, the Cuban characteristics will probably be completely subverted through time.

Today the Cuban crocodile feeds mainly upon fish and turtles, its large, flattened rear teeth crushing the turtle's shell very easily. The high walk of the Cuban crocodile shows that it probably hunted more on land in the past than it does today. Then those large rear teeth would have been used for crushing bone. Very little is known about the nest and egg laying of the Cuban crocodile but, as most other crocodiles pile up vegetation for a nest, it is probably safe to assume that this one does also. The eggs are 7.5 centimetres (3 inches) in length by 5 centimetres (2 inches) in diameter.

Morelet's crocodiles are found only on the Caribbean side of Central America, from Mexico down to Guatemala. They are a freshwater species, although they may occasionally be found in brackish coastal regions.

The Cuban crocodile has an extremely limited range, now found only in the Zapata Swamp in Cuba. Its numbers have been greatly reduced, more by the destruction of its habitat than by hunting.

The Orinoco Crocodile

The Orinoco crocodile, *Crocodylus inter-medius*, inhabits only the Orinoco River drainage basin in Venezuela and the Meta River drainage basin in Colombia. It is a large crocodile, measuring 5 metres (16 1/2 feet) or more with somewhat questionable records of 7 metres (22 feet) from the "good old days" not uncommon.

Because the crocodile has no osteoderms on its belly, and is large in size, its hide was in great demand for leather. In the heyday of the market hunter, from 1925 to 1935, fortunes were made and hundreds of thousands of these crocodiles were killed. Today they are given a measure of protection and it is no longer feasible to hunt them. It is estimated that there are less than fifteen hundred of this species left in the wild.

The female digs a hole on a riverbank that is above the flood-stage level. Here she deposits thirty to forty eggs and covers them up. She takes up a sentry post a short distance away to ward off such predators as the terid lizards and black vultures. After two months or so, the eggs hatch. The hatchlings feed mainly upon beetles, snails, crabs, and invertebrates. Its long,

The large size of the Orinoco crocodile allows it to feed upon animals as large as the capybara, the largest rodent in the world. The Orinocos have been known to attack man, but this is a rare occurrence.

The Orinoco crocodile inhabits the upland reaches of the Orinoco River in both Venezuela and Colombia. They have been found in both Trinidad and Grenada after being washed out to sea during floods.

narrow snout is indicative of its diet of fish. The adults feed mainly upon fish, birds, and the capybara. These big rodents often weigh up to one hundred pounds and provide a good food source. There are no authenticated reports of this crocodile attacking humans.

During periods of flooding, this crocodile leaves the Orinoco River and travels overland to nearby quiet lakes and ponds. As the waters recede after the rainy season, the crocs go back to the deeper river. There are records of this crocodile being swept out to sea on masses of vegetation during the high flood period and ending up on the offshore islands of Trinidad and Grenada.

Note that only three of the toes on the front foot of this Orinoco crocodile have toenails as claws. These nails allow the crocodile to get a good grip on a muddy riverbank and aid in digging its nest.

The Orinoco crocodile grows to a length of up to 6 metres (20 feet) and, as their hides are used extensively for leather, they have been heavily hunted almost to the point of extinction. Captive breeding programmes are being pursued.

Previous page: *Ordinarily, crocodiles will tolerate the close presence of others of the same species. However, intraspecies conflict does occur during the mating season in competition for favoured nesting sites and over food. Scars caused by fighting are often seen.*

Many ducks, geese, and wading birds coexist safely in the same habitat as the Nile crocodile. However, these Egyptian geese keep a watchful eye on the crocodiles because the crocodiles feed upon any goose that is not vigilant.

The Nile Crocodile

I have seen the Nile crocodile, *Crocodylus niloticus*, stacked up like cordwood on the riverbank below Murchison's Falls in Uganda. These crocodiles were guarded carefully by the wardens of the park. Elsewhere, their population has been greatly reduced by market hunting, with three million hides being taken between 1950 and 1980. In some other areas, such as Lake Turkana in Kenya, many of the crocs are trapped and drown in fishermen's gill nets.

In Natal, so much water has been removed from Lake St. Lucia for agricultural irrigation and the lake has become so saline that the crocodiles are dying. While no one wants to see a species exterminated, the native people are very glad to see the population of this crocodile greatly diminished. The Nile crocodile is a fearsome man-eater and it is estimated that it kills about three hundred people per year, even today. The native women wash their clothes by sitting in the rivers, often facing the bank, and usually don't see the crocodile that takes them.

It is a large crocodile, with many being over 5 metres (16 1/2 feet) in length. In 1905 a monster Nile crocodile was killed in Tanzania that measured over 6.5 metres (21 feet) and weighed about 1035 kilogrammes (2,300 pounds). A more recent leviathan taken in 1953 in Uganda measured 5.9 metres (19 1/2 feet) in length and more than 2 metres (6.6 feet) in heart girth.

While photographing the crocodiles at Murchison's Falls, a rope accidentally became entangled around our launch's propeller. One of the natives dove overboard and cut the propeller free. There is no way that I would have volunteered for that job with all those

The Nile crocodile and hippopotamus live in close proximity to one another. Although this hippo is too large to be in danger from the crocodile, baby hippos are frequently attacked and sometimes killed by crocodiles.

The fourth tooth on either side of a crocodile's lower jaw fits into a corresponding hole in the upper jaw so that the tip of the tooth protrudes through. This protrusion can be seen when the crocodile closes its mouth completely.

Lying motionless at the edge of the water, crocodiles wait for prey to come and drink. With a startlingly swift lunge, this crocodile has seised an impala and pulled it into the water to drown.

The crocodile's teeth are conical in shape and are designed for grasping its prey. Lacking shearing or grinding teeth, the crocodile tears its prey into chunks small enough to swallow by rolling over quickly in the water and pulling the prey's limbs loose from its body.

Large fish are the Nile crocodile's main dietary staple. The warm water in which these creatures are found produces an enormous amount of vegetative plankton that the fish feed upon and grow large very quickly.

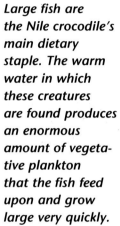

In digging its nest, the crocodile may use either its fore or hind feet. The broad surface and strong nails of the feet make them effective shovels. The nest will be located in the dry sand of a riverbank, above the high-water level.

The mother crocodile must protect her hatchlings because they are small enough, about 25 centimetres (10 inches) in length, to be preyed upon by larger wading birds that would swallow them whole.

The female crocodile will lay between fifty and sixty of her leathery-shelled eggs at one time. She will then cover them over with sand and allow the ambient temperature to heat the sand to hatch them. She will remain nearby to keep predators at a distance.

toothy denizens piled up on the bank. I will add that not one of the crocs even stirred to enter the water. During Idi Amin's fearsome rule of Uganda in the 1970s, he disposed of the bodies of his political enemies by feeding them to the Murchison's crocodiles.

The adult crocodiles lie in the water and wait for prey species to come and drink. Then, with a sudden lunge, amid a cascade of water they spring forward to grasp the prey and pull it into the water to drown. They will take birds of any and all sizes and animals up to the size of a horse or giraffe. I have seen where the crocs had killed so many wildebeests, at the Mara River crossing in Kenya, that they couldn't eat them all.

Despite the taking of birds as prey, a symbiotic relationship has developed between the crocodiles and the African spur-winged plover and the thicknee. This was first written up by Herodotus almost 2500 years ago. He wrote that as the Nile crocodile lay with its mouth open, these two species of birds would pick leeches and food particles from between the teeth of the crocodile. This came to be regarded as a myth because so much of what this Greek historian wrote proved to be groundless. However, this commensal relationship has been documented by modern-day researchers.

This crocodile's nest is an excavated hole dug in a riverbank or sandbar above the high-water level. Fifty to sixty eggs may be laid and the nest will be guarded by the female and sometimes by the male as well. I have seen 1.5-metre (5-foot) monitor lizards in the same vicinity as these huge saurians, but have not witnessed them digging up the eggs. The Nile crocodile is found throughout most of Africa except for the northwest desert and the southern mountain areas.

This baby Nile crocodile has just cut its way out of the egg. Note that because of its leathery composition, the eggshell has been peeled back instead of cracking into small pieces, as would the more calcium-rich, brittle eggshell of a bird.

The African Caiman

The African slender-snouted caiman, *Crocodylus cataphractus*, is a little-known crocodile, usually solitary and very shy. It does little or no basking and inhabits a deep jungle environment so that it is seldom seen. It is found in all of the West African countries bordering the Atlantic Ocean from Senegal south to Angola. It prefers the quiet waters of slow-flowing rivers, lakes, and ponds. They average 2.5 metres (8 feet) in length, with a really big one being half again as large. Their long, slender snout and body fit their aquatic life and they feed heavily upon fish, although they also feed upon small mammals and birds.

At egg-laying time, the female piles up a nest of vegetation, mainly forest tree leaves, on the edge of a riverbank. She lays a small clutch of eggs, averaging sixteen. This small clutch size shows that these crocodiles are subject to little predation because each species lays eggs enough to keep their population stable. She will help the young to get out of the nest when they hatch and grunt to call her.

The African Dwarf Crocodile

There is scientific disagreement as to whether the West African dwarf crocodile, *Osteolaemus tetraspis*, is one species or if it should be broken down into two species.

This species is found in Sierra Leone, Guinea, Ghana, Togo, Nigeria, Cameroon, and Gabon. A second species, or subspecies, has been dubbed the Congo dwarf crocodile, *Osteoblepharon osborni*.

These crocodiles are distinguished by their small size of about 1.5 metres (5 feet). There are records of some that have reached a length of 1.8 metres (6 feet), but that is exceedingly rare. Another characteristic is the crocodile's upturned nose.

Their small size makes them inoffensive to man and their ventral osteoderms make their hides unfit for leather, so they have been relatively unmolested. They are freshwater crocodiles and are found in the rivers, ponds, and lakes of the jungle region. Not a great deal is known of their habits and, although their diet is primarily fish, it is believed that they secure some of their food on land, as do the monitors and iguanas. They seldom bask on riverbanks or sandbars and are not really seen that often as they are most active under the cover of darkness. It is known that, when they are disturbed, they will seek refuge in tunnels that they dig in riverbanks.

The nest is a mound of vegetation piled up by the female in which she deposits her ten to fifteen eggs. She guards the nest against predators for the three months that it takes the eggs to hatch.

The African slender-snouted caiman is found along the western coast of Africa from Senegal south to Angola. It is found inland as far as Central African Republic and Zaire.

The heavy osteoderms on most of the skin of the West African dwarf crocodile render its skin useless to hide hunters. Their lack of market value gives these reptiles substantial protection against poachers.

The dwarf crocodile is well named, as it is the smallest member of the crocodilian family. A really big adult may measure up to 1.8 metres (6 feet) in length.

INDO-PACIFIC CROCODILES

The Saltwater Crocodile

The Indo-Pacific or saltwater crocodile, *Crocodylus porosus*, is the largest and most fearsome of all of the crocodilians. One killed in Australia's Northwest Territory in June 1960 measured 6.15 metres (20 feet, 2 inches) in length. In 1962, another one of these crocodiles was killed in the Territory that measured just 6 metres (20 feet), but weighed an incredible 1088 kilogrammes (2,418 pounds). The largest crocodile reported was not killed, but the sandbar on which it rested was measured by James Montgomery on the Segama River in Borneo in the 1920s. It was estimated that the crocodile was 10 metres (33 feet) long. A crocodile now living in the

In courtship, the male saltwater crocodile will caress the female by rubbing his head over her back and along her flanks. Thus stimulated, the female will more readily accept the male for copulation.

Although this male saltwater crocodile is clasping the female in the dorso-ventral copulation position assumed by most animals, he will have to get her to either twist or turn her body so that they will be in the ventral-ventral position in order to copulate successfully.

Bhitarkanika Sanctuary in Orissa, India, is estimated to be 7 metres (23 feet) in length.

The Indo-Pacific crocodile inhabits an area encompassing the lower tip of India to the Philippines, all of Indonesia and surrounding islands, and northern Australia. In that vast territory, it is estimated that this crocodile kills at least one thousand people each year.

The greatest carnage done by these crocodiles occurred toward the end of World War II. The British, in retaking Burma, had pushed a force of over one thousand Japanese soldiers to the coast. The Japanese had expected to be picked up by one of their ships and evacuated. However, because of British ships patrolling just off the coast, the Japanese rescue ship was turned back. The Japanese soldiers fled into a large mangrove swamp between Burma and Romree Island. During the night the Indo-Pacific crocodiles attacked and, by morning, only twenty Japanese were still alive.

The Indo-Pacific crocodile feeds upon fish but, like the Nile crocodile, it can catch mammals up to the size of water buffaloes. It stealthily sneaks closer and closer until, within striking distance, it charges out of the water, grasps its prey, and pulls it into

the water to drown. This crocodile is also called the saltwater crocodile because it is found primarily in saltwater or brackish areas. Its salt glands are well developed and it can ingest saltwater with no harmful effects. However, this crocodile will travel many kilometres up freshwater rivers and streams. The one I encountered in Australia was about 48 kilometres (30 miles) up the Alligator River from the ocean.

In keeping with their large size, these crocs make a nest that may be 2.5 metres (8 feet) across and 91 centimetres (3 feet) in height. The nest is made of piled-up vegetation liberally mixed with mud. As many as ninety eggs have been found in one nest. Incubation takes three months, with the female guarding against predators. Due to the mud hardening, the female is needed to help the young escape from the nest.

The most fearsome of all the crocodiles are the large Indo-Pacific, or saltwater, crocodiles. It is reported that this crocodile may be responsible for killing as many as one thousand people each year over its vast range.

The mugger crocodile is the most common crocodile found on the Indian subcontinent. It is also known as the "marsh crocodile" as it favours the shallow areas of freshwater rivers, ponds, and lakes.

The Mugger Crocodile

The mugger crocodile, *Crocodylus palustris*, is the sacred crocodile of India. It is found in India, Nepal, Pakistan, Iran, and Sri Lanka. Most males will average 1.8 to 2.4 metres (6-8 feet) in length with really big ones reaching 4 metres (13 feet).

The mugger has the same broad snout as the alligators. It, too, is a marsh-dwelling creature. In fact the "palustris" in its name means "of the marshes". It prefers fresh water but occasionally will be found in estuaries. Like the alligator, the mugger is an opportunistic feeder, eating mainly fish but also eating any turtles, snakes, birds, and small mammals that it can find. It does not attack man. The human birthrate of the area in which the mugger is found is very high and, as the human population increases, all types of wildlife, the mug-ger included, are greatly reduced. Captive breeding programmes are under way in several of the countries involved in an effort to prevent the loss of that species.

The nest is simply a hole dug in a riverbank by the female in the months of February and March. Thirty eggs comprise the average clutch, which takes about sixty-five days to hatch.

The New Guinea Crocodile

The New Guinea crocodile, *Crocodylus noureguineae*, was not confirmed as a distinct species until 1938. New Guinea has a high mountain range running lengthwise through the island and this mountain has separated this species into two subspecies. As this crocodile is a freshwater species, it will not swim around the land mass and no interbreeding between the north/south subspecies is known to occur. This crocodile grows to a length of 4 metres (13 feet). They have been hunted extensively for their hides so that their population is greatly reduced.

This species prefers the spacious swamplands found at the lower elevations. In times of drought, these crocodiles will seek refuge in the deeper rivers. They are seldom seen because they are almost strictly nocturnal. It is known that it feeds upon fish, amphibians, reptiles, and water birds. Being a very shy creature, it is not a threat to man.

The nest is a mound of vegetation piled up at the edge of the dense jungle just high enough above the water to be above flood stage. Their nests have also been found built

This mugger crocodile has just caught an axis, or chittal, deer when it came down to drink. Unable to sever a leg with its teeth, the crocodile will tear off a leg of the deer by rolling its body rapidly in the water.

An enormous mugger crocodile is chasing off a smaller crocodile from the axis deer which it has killed. In the wild, the larger specimens of any species will be dominant, which gives them the first chance at any available food.

Although crocodilians usually tolerate those of their own kind, large ones do occasionally eat smaller ones. This mugger crocodile is being chased by a much larger one.

A dwarf population has been found among Johnston's freshwater crocodiles. These smaller crocodiles grow to a length of about 1.6 metres (5 feet) and are generally much darker in colouration than their normal-sized kin.

up on floating mats of vegetation. The female lays about thirty eggs and stays in the vicinity to guard the nest. Being shy, she will not defend the nest if a man appears. The young hatch in a period of twelve weeks, with both the male and the female taking the hatchlings to water. Although the adults are seldom seen basking, the young need the warmth of the sun and spend considerable time lying in the sunshine. This is important because, as the sun raises the baby crocodile's body temperature, it stimulates the baby to feed.

Johnston's Crocodile

The Johnston's crocodile, *Crocodylus johnstoni*, is better known as the Australian freshwater crocodile. As the Indo-Pacific saltwater crocodile is frequently found kilometres from

The Johnston's freshwater crocodile is found only in the northern region of Australia. This crocodile is smaller in size the farther upstream it is found, due to a decreasing supply of food. It may occasionally be found in coastal marshes.

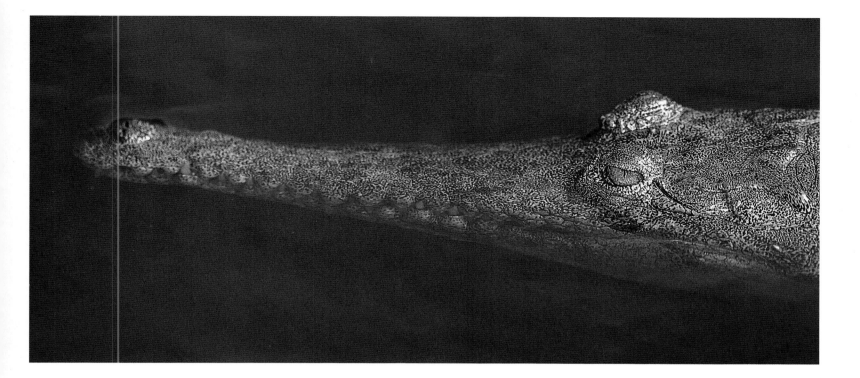

the coast, living in fresh water, the Johnston's crocodile can sometimes be found in brackish esturine areas. It is found across the northern edge of Australia. Its long, tapered nose shows that it is primarily aquatic, feeding mainly upon fish, amphibians, turtles, and occasionally birds and small mammals. Although it grows to a length of 3 metres (10 feet), it is not aggressive toward man. In some areas there are dwarf populations of this crocodile. It is believed that it is the periodic shortage of food during the drought season that has produced these smaller crocodiles as an adaptation. Quite logically, the crocodiles become smaller the closer you get to the headwaters of any of the rivers. As there is a lessening of food, there is a lessening of crocodilian growth.

The females do not build a mound as a nest, but simply dig a hole in the riverbank. Often a large number of females will nest in one general area. This could result from a lack of suitable nesting sites as much as from sociability. The clutches are small, with twelve to eighteen eggs being the norm. The eggs hatch

Despite growing to a length of about 10 feet (3 metres), the Johnston's freshwater crocodile is not considered to be a threat to man. Its range sometimes overlaps that of the saltwater crocodile which often is a man-eater.

in about three months. Although the eggs are often preyed upon by monitor lizards, the female is not a particularly good guardian.

The Philippine Crocodile

The Philippine crocodile, *Crocodylus mindorensis*, is an exceedingly rare species. Whereas it was formerly found on a number of the Philippine Islands, the remnant population, believed to be less than five hundred individuals, is now centred on the island of Mindanao and the Sulu Archipelago. The combination of overhunting for its skins and destruction and drainage of its habitat for agriculture has severely endangered this species. There are several captive breeding programmes under way at the present time in a concerted effort to prevent the extinction of this crocodile.

Although the Philippine crocodile attains a length of up to 3 metres (10 feet), it is shy and not aggressive toward man. These are mound-building crocodiles, with the female piling up vegetation. Again, the clutches are small, with ten to twelve eggs being the average. The small clutch size also is a deterrent to rapid population growth. Incubation of the eggs takes twelve weeks, with the female in constant attendance. This is a freshwater species, found in both the rivers and lakes, where it feeds mainly upon fish. Occasional birds and small mammals are also taken.

The long, thin snout of the Johnston's freshwater crocodile is indicative of the fact that it feeds primarily upon fish. The narrow snout allows it to more easily slash sideways through the water.

The Siamese Crocodile

The Siamese crocodile, *Crocodylus siamensis*, is another crocodile on the verge of extinction in the wild, primarily because it was hunted so heavily for its hide. This crocodile also suffers the disadvantage of looking so much like the Indo-Pacific crocodile that it was killed because it was mistaken for the latter. While the Siamese crocodile is not aggressive toward man and the Indo-Pacific crocodile is, to most people "a crocodile is a crocodile" and the relatively harmless Siamese crocs were killed out of fear of the latter species.

At one time this crocodile, which lives primarily in fresh water but also occasionally in brackish water, the same habitat as the Indo-Pacific crocodile, was found in Vietnam, Cambodia, Thailand, Laos, and the Malay Peninsula. Today, the only wild population, which numbers about fifty individuals, is found at a reservoir in the Nakhon Province in Thailand.

The female lays her twenty to forty eggs in a mound of vegetation. She guards the eggs during the eleven-week incubation period and helps the hatchlings to emerge from the nest. The young feed upon aquatic insects and small fish. The adults feed mainly upon fish, supplementing their diet with whatever waterfowl and small mammals that they can capture.

The Siamese crocodile is becoming extremely rare in the wild. The wild population has been reduced to about fifty individuals which are found only on the Bung Boraphet in Thailand.

The False Gharial

The false gharial, *Tomistoma schlegelii*, is a freshwater crocodile that has the long, very thin snout of the true gharial, or gavial. But unlike the true gharial, this crocodile has a stout body. It grows to a length of about 1.8 metres (6 feet) and is harmless to man. The false gharial is an endangered species, with a few wild populations found only on the Malay Peninsula, Sumatra, and Borneo. The loss of habitat is the prime reason for the reduction in the numbers of this crocodile.

The fact that, after the female lays her eggs in a mound of vegetation, she does not guard them leaves the nest subject to heavy predation. Feral hogs and even those kept under domestication by the locals wreak havoc on the nests and, if discovered, all fifty to sixty eggs will be eaten.

This crocodile received its name of false gharial because of its extremely slim, long snout which is the identifying characteristic of the true gharial. It also has a heavier, more compact body than does the true gharial.

The false gharial, or gavial, is also called the Tomistoma, from its latin name. It is really a freshwater crocodile living in the Malaysia region of the South Pacific and is not related to the gharial of the Asian mainland.

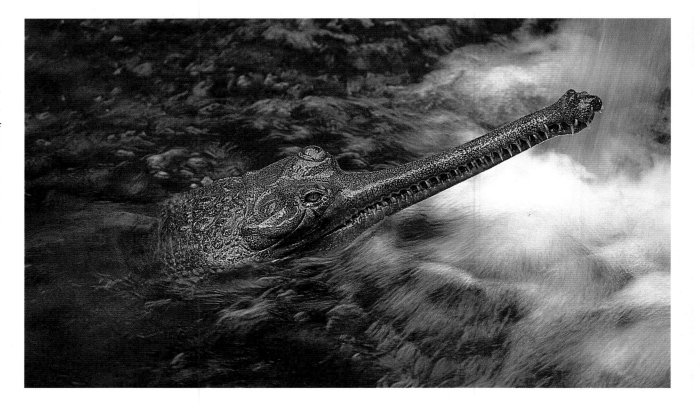

The gharial can be found from India to Laos. Their population has been greatly reduced both by the destruction of their habitat and by overhunting. Hunting gharials was once the sport of royalty in India.

The long, thin, extremely toothy snout of the gharial is its most distinguishing characteristic. It is also an indication that the gharial feeds mainly upon fish. The narrow snout allows the gharial to move through the water, slashing sideways or lunging forward, very easily.

The Gharial

The gharial, or gavial, *Gavialis gangeticus*, is a crocodilian, but it is the only species in its own family. As its Latin name reveals, the gharial is a creature of the Ganges, Chambal, and Brahmaputra rivers in India and the Rapti-Narayani River in Nepal. The gharial cannot be mistaken for any of the other crocodilians due to its long, slim body, extremely long, thin snout, and its sharply rear-curving teeth.

They do grow to a large size, with one being shot that measured 6.5 metres (21 feet). They feed almost exclusively upon fish and their thinness in both snout and body allow them to move very quickly through the water. The thin snout is often swung sideways, like a scythe, through the water.

It is not known if the female makes a mound nest or, as is more commonly suspected, digs a hole in the sand. Captive females have been known to lay about forty eggs. The gharials do not attack humans. They have been hunted for the leather market and their eggs are often used for food by the natives. Unfortunately, much of the Asian pharmacopeia is based on using various parts of wild creatures. Parts of gharial snouts are supposed to have aphrodisiac qualities.

India has a high birth rate. Much destruction of habitat accompanies a human population explosion, and the gharials have suffered because of this. Captive breeding programmes are under way to save this species from extinction.

The gharials, or gavials, are very large crocodiles, some having reached a length of 7 metres (23 feet). Despite its large size, it is not known to be aggressive toward man.

INDEX

*Page numbers in **bold-face** type indicate photo captions.*